Poetic Reflections

Diane Alexy

Also by Diane Alexy

POEMS FROM MY SOUL
TAKE MY HAND: Poetry and Photography

Poetic Reflections

Copyright © 2017 Diane Alexy

All rights reserved.

ISBN: 1546703969
ISBN-13: 978-1546703969

Poetic Reflections

♦ POEMS ♦

Nature

End of Day	Page 3
Full Moon	Page 4
Dawn's Fireflies	Page 5
The Nature of Nature	Page 6
Pink Petals	Page 7
Spring Renewal	Page 8
Spring Song	Page 9
Stolen Gold	Page 10
December	Page 11

Spiritual

If Only	Page 15
The Lesson	Page 16
Now	Page 17
Regret	Page 18
Darkened Heart	Page 19
Bad News	Page 20
Gratitude	Page 21

♦ POEMS ♦

Spiritual (continued)

Forever	Page 22
Inner Strength	Page 23
Heaven on Earth	Page 24
My Voice	Page 25
Social Darkness	Page 26
Released	Page 27
Solace	Page 28
The Voice of a Child's Soul	Page 29
Our Cosmic Connection	Page 30
Gaining Joy	Page 31
Letting Go	Pages 32-33

Childhood

Dovidenia	Page 37
Childhood Memories of the Sea	Page 38
Nana's Garden	Page 39

About the Poet — Page 41

I dedicate this book to Harry Castiglione. Harry was a dear friend and father figure—a remarkable man who was beloved of family and friends. He welcomed me into his heart and honored me with the gift of his great love and care. When his son described him as being "as close to a saint as any man could be," I could only wholeheartedly agree with this wonderful tribute. I feel blessed to have known his beautiful spirit, to have felt the joy of loving him deeply, and to have been loved so tenderly in return.

Poetic Reflections

I reflect on the past and present
I've pondered the future too
Please join my soul on this journey
Through these poems I share with you

Diane Alexy

End of Day

The sun has set; light fades away
After too brief a vast display

Of colors bright—breathtaking hues
That filled the sky with pinks and blues

With purple too and golden tone
Of heaven's vista just on loan

Peace then descends at end of day
Its grand finale now replayed

Full Moon

I looked up out the window
It was the dark of night
And there before delighted eyes
A full moon beamed so bright

The biggest moon I'd ever seen
Now blazed in ghostly white
"Luna piena" came to mind
Italian for this sight

How beautiful the sky appeared
With moon and stars alight
When brilliant jewels of the night sky
Adorned the darkened height

Dawn's Fireflies

One magical past summer's night
A "million" fireflies took flight
Creating a most wondrous sight
They filled the earth with flares of light

I would have loved to see the way
That nature awed Dawn on that day
With such a joyful, vast display
That she still treasures to this day

The Nature of Nature

Nature can be our greatest gift
It moors us when we feel adrift

A full moon in a darkened sky
Provides us with a natural high

The perfume from a sweet red rose
Is straight from heaven I propose

Lapping shores can soothe our soul
And nature's rhythms make us whole

But mother nature can be cruel
And in a heartless manner rule

When all we have is cut to naught
Her brutal lesson is well-taught

I've often pondered re this rift—
Nature as ruthless and a gift

We can but hope that in this life
To know her beauty, not her strife

Pink Petals

Pink petals flit like butterflies
  from blooming cherry trees
    the frilly blossoms forced apart
     now by a warm spring breeze

It's sad these lovely blooms depart
  so soon after their birth
    ending their joyful, brief stay here
     as petals on the earth

Spring Renewal

The trees are majestic once again and barren winter is forgotten. Exquisite beauty unfolds where once cold and naked branches waited. Having endured, now reborn, they are lush with consummate blossoms—treasures of spring that create joy and a feeling of hope within our hearts.

Spring Song

Sweet springtime bursts with thriving life
As bleakness fades away

The trees explode with growing buds
Green leaves are on their way

Such vibrant flowers in gardens bloom
Now bathed in sunlit rays

Souls winter-weary sing along
With the song that springtime plays

Stolen Gold

Fall trees are rich with leaves of gold
  Providing us with pleasure
    But branches will turn sadly bare
      When cold winds steal the treasure

December

The raging winds speak of the cold
December's chill is here
I mourn the loss of painted leaves
Too quick to disappear

And even more I miss the green
Bare branches are austere
Their stark sight leaves me yearning for
Their spring wardrobe to wear

Spiritual

If Only

If only the sky were a sweet pink
That's my favorite color you know
And if only the earth came in purple
How pretty a garden would grow

But the sky is a beautiful soft blue
And the brown of the earth is just fine
So instead of my thinking "if only"
Contented I'll be and not pine…

But if only I had great riches
Wouldn't life then be perfect today?
Ah, but if I enjoy what I do have
Joy won't be "if only-ed" away

The Lesson

I learned an impressive lesson
About worrying the other day
Something serious had happened
And I started then to pray

For bad luck to turn around
And my panic to go away
But my soul could not let worry go
And trembled in dismay

Then the unexpected happened
And my plight had been resolved
And almost like a miracle
My problem was now solved

The relief I felt was massive
Almost like I'd been reborn
And after this bad incident
I've to myself now sworn

To stop worrying about the things
That could then go awry
Taking steps to preclude problems
But not wolf re trials cry

Something dreadful rarely happens
And to fret will cause distress
Relief from anguish felt so good
I've now vowed to worry less

Now

It's time to take the time to do
And not just pass the days
Pondering if the dreams you hold
Will somehow come your way

It's time to take your dearest wish
And on it now to act
It's time to do what can be done
To turn your dream to fact

Regret

We have all done things we wish we could take back and do again. Weighed down by regret, we beat ourselves up about what we should and could have done. But feeling bad about ourselves will not change the past and only magnifies our remorse by involving the present in our past self-discontent. So forgive yourself, vow to be wiser in the future, and live well now without the burden of the weight of regretfulness.

Darkened Heart

Dawn relieved the long night's dark
Through sleepless hours passed
But the shadow still remained
That grieving long had cast

Which tainted every bitter breath
I managed to sustain
Dawn relieved the dark of night
But not the dark of pain

Bad News

Heartbroken I just heard the news
Of yet more troubled souls who'd choose
Vast violence to express their hate
Where innocents would meet their fate

This news is hard to comprehend
The loss of life a tragedy
It makes no sense to us because
Its source is rank insanity

Where does the answer to this lie?
How will we ever gain relief
From violent acts of lunatics
Who have resolved to cause us grief?

Gratitude

Thank you, Lord, for skies of blue
And love in life that's warm and true

Thank you for your gift of birth
And for my treasured time on earth

Thank you for renewal in spring
And for the beauty it will bring

Many thanks for flowers bright
And days of summer's brilliant light

Thanks when autumn is ablaze
And trees so dazzling fill our days

Many thanks for winters white
When flakes of lacy snow delight

Lord, with grateful heart I pray
In thanks for blessings every day

Forever

Our spirits are bound forever
You are mine and I am yours
As night sky and moon are coupled
As are rushing waves and shore

You showed me what true love is
When others would cede this role
You blessed me with your kindness
You saved my endangered soul

And when my time on earth ends
And heaven is also my home
Since bonds of love forever live
Together our souls will roam

Inner Strength

Night falls upon the winter's day
The earth now dark and cold
But even such great bitterness
Cannot then pierce my soul

The warmth and strength of our great love
Has sheltered my deep core
Remaining still, though you are gone,
And grace this world no more

Heaven on Earth

Taking wing to the beach one autumn day
I tossed pieces of fragrant bread to the seabirds
Who fluttered excitedly above me
Their white feathers dazzling celestially
While the song of the surf soothed eternally
And I felt as close to heaven as I could be

Then I met him and in the warmth of his hand
The light in his eyes shining down on me
The smile on his countenance caressing me
The song in my heart playing tenderly
In the beauty and the magic of love
I discovered what heaven truly meant to me

My Voice

My heart and soul live in my words
My poet's voice speaks out
With righteous anger when it knows
It's time with rage to shout

It also knows that nature's due
Words fashioned to extol
Its wonder and its majesty
Which nourishes the soul

My voice speaks often of the love
That flows deep in my core
It is the reason we are here
Without it we are poor

My soul has known the fear of hurt
My voice speaks of the dark
That many lives have to endure
Which leaves its tragic mark

My voice speaks of the sorrow reaped
From having been betrayed
By those who didn't love and care
Whose malice bred dismay

My voice speaks of abiding faith
In God's love I believe
I sense the sacred in my soul
And heaven I perceive

Social Darkness

The day can be so lovely
With sun and cloudless skies
Then rapidly turn ugly
When social kindness dies

And someone who you're joining
To share some friendly time
Begins to give free rein to
Whatever's on his mind

No matter how offensive
The words he picks to say
How negative and thoughtless
It is to speak this way

He feels somehow self-righteous
And sometimes even brags
That his ideas are better
And on you he then rags

It grieves a caring heart when
A sunny day turns gray
Because a so-called "friend"
Takes the social joy away

Released

Like the bird I see soaring against the blue and white of the morning sky, my soul flies free. Now that I have ended the burden you had become I feel released, knowing that you will never again be allowed to subject my spirit to the rage that you cannot control.

Solace

Life can sometimes bring unwanted changes and one's heart can long for happiness lost. There is solace in knowing that even though a change has now brought diminished joy, there is always hope that at any moment further change will lead to contentment even greater than one has ever known before.

The Voice of a Child's Soul

The best thing is a mommy
Who loves me every day
And when I fall and scrape my knee
She hugs the hurt away

The best thing is a mommy
To love with all my heart
And to wish on Mother's Day
That we would never part

It's great to have a mommy
To be there when my fears
Scare me in the dark of night
To kiss away my tears

But why God does my mommy
Fill every day with fear
And by the way she hurts me
Tells me she doesn't care?

The best thing is a mommy
Who'll love me every day
And for such a mommy, God,
Each day to you I'll pray

Our Cosmic Connection

We're part of nature's rhythms
We flow with the vast seas
We ascend with every sunrise
And renew with lush spring trees

We're part of God's creation
And with the earth we're one
We're warmed by cosmic energy
Just like the golden sun

And when our broken bodies
Can earth no longer roam
The force that is our spirit
Lives on in its new home

Gaining Joy

When things go wrong
  we fret and fume
    in most intensive ways

I here propose
  when things go right
    we laud our lucky days

When times are good
  and we are blessed
    to have escaped life's fray

With passion we
  should celebrate
    that nothing's gone astray

When fate is good
  and we applaud
    we'll gain joy in our day

Letting Go

I think I can let go now
  The time has come to try
    To accept this awful fate
      And cease to question why

You had to go away
  And leave me here in tears
    My heart wrenched by your loss
      And ever-present fears

Of never being loved
  And loving as I had
    Of being left alone
      My soul forever sad

Like magnets drawn together
  In natural reaction
    We had a strong and tender
      Deeply felt attraction

When you touched me gently
  I felt so warm inside
    Your caring, loving feelings
      You'd openly confide

Letting Go (continued)

I loved you very deeply
  I know I always will
    True love can never die
      And lives within me still

Your spirit filled with pure light
  Was decent, warm and kind
    On earth another shining soul
      Like yours is hard to find

Your memory is cherished
  And never will depart
    Its truth and beauty dwelling
      Undying in my heart

Dovidenia

Nana would say "Dovidenia," which is Slovak for "see you next time." And each next time was as treasured and wonderful as the time before. But one day, so very long ago, there was no next time and that beautiful word from such a loving soul would never be spoken again. But it was never forgotten and neither was the bond of true love held within my heart that shaped me and sustained me. And so, my beloved nana, I say to you Dovidenia—see you next time—when our souls will meet again in a place far better than what this world has now become.

Childhood Memories of the Sea

I love the scent of salty sea
That conjures happy memory

Of childhood play upon the shore
Of rocks and sea shells to explore

Of sun-warmed sand between my toes
Of letting go of earthly woes

Of riding on the pounding waves
In an inner tube and feeling brave

And since my nana's there with me
My soul's as blessed as it could be

Nana's Garden

My true memory transports me to this perfect place and again I feel the deep peace and innocence of a sleepy kitten. I am back, where among the roses and the pansies and the warm soothing sun, hope and infinite love fill my tender heart. This is the sentiment of my cherished youth, but also how I desire to define my present and the golden years of life yet to come.

About the Poet

In September of 2012, Diane was honored to be awarded a rare old book of poetry by the director of Nomad's Choir on the day she read as a new poet to this group. Diane has since had several of her poems published in the *Nomad's Choir Poetry Journal*.

In May of 2013, she was Poet of the Month at The New York Poetry Forum.

Diane has also been privileged to read her poetry to members of the Women's Welsh New York City Club and to have had her poems published in the group's monthly newsletters. One of her nature photographs was posted on the Club's website.

Diane has had her poetry published in the 2017 *7 Train Anthology* and most recently in the June-July 2017 issue of *Creations Magazine*.

Made in the USA
Lexington, KY
04 October 2017